FINGERPICKING ROCK

ISBN 978-0-634-09892-5

HAL•LEONARD®
CORPORATION
7777 W. BLUEMOUND RD. P.O. BOX 13819 MILWAUKEE, WI 53213

Visit Hal Leonard Online at
www.halleonard.com

INTRODUCTION TO FINGERSTYLE GUITAR

Fingerstyle (a.k.a. fingerpicking) is a guitar technique that means you literally pick the strings with your right-hand fingers and thumb. This contrasts with the conventional technique of strumming and playing single notes with a pick (a.k.a. flatpicking). For fingerpicking, you can use any type of guitar: acoustic steel-string, nylon-string classical, or electric.

THE RIGHT HAND

The most common right-hand position is shown below:

Use a high wrist; arch your palm as if you were holding a ping-pong ball. Keep the thumb outside and away from the fingers, and let the fingers do the work rather than lifting your whole hand.

The thumb generally plucks the bottom strings with downstrokes on the left side of the thumb and thumbnail. The other fingers pluck the higher strings using upstrokes with the fleshy tip of the fingers and fingernails. The thumb and fingers should pluck one string per stroke and not brush over several strings.

Another picking option you may choose to use is called **hybrid picking** (a.k.a. plectrum-style fingerpicking). Here, the pick is usually held between the thumb and first finger, and the three remaining fingers are assigned to pluck the higher strings.

THE LEFT HAND

The left-hand fingers are numbered 1 through 4:

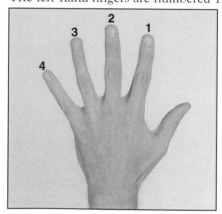

Be sure to keep your fingers arched, with each joint bent; if they flatten out across the strings, they will deaden the sound when you fingerpick. As a general rule, let the strings ring as long as possible when playing fingerstyle.

Come Sail Away

Words and Music by Dennis DeYoung

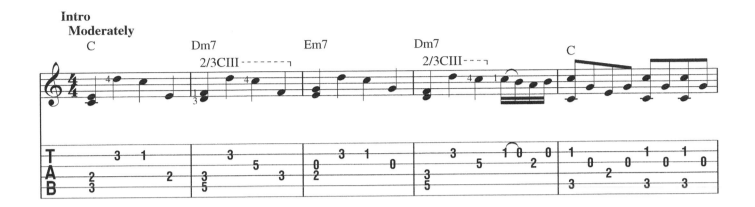

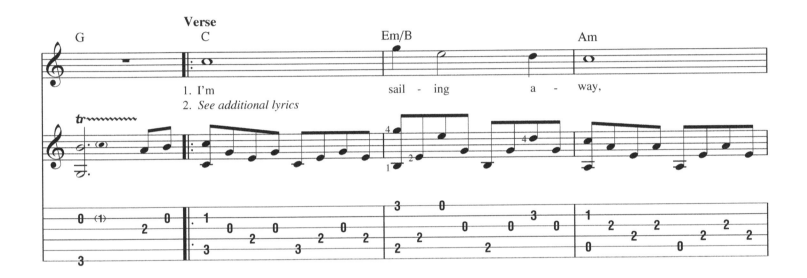

shore. _____ And I'll try, oh Lord, I'll __ try

to car - ry on.

Interlude

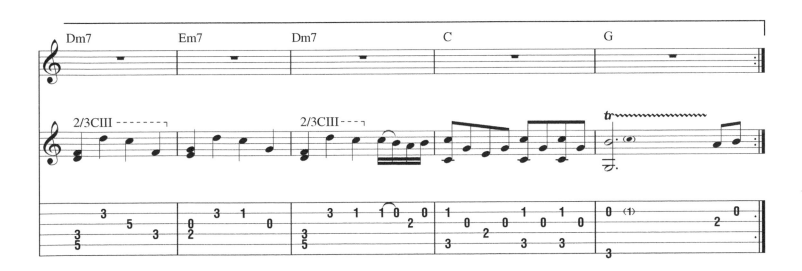

Additional Lyrics

2. I look to the sea,
   Reflections in the waves spark my memory.
   Some happy, some sad.
   I think of childhood friends and the dreams we had.
   We live happily together, so the story goes.
   But somehow we missed out on a pot of gold.
   But we'll try best that we can to carry on.

Pre-Chorus I thought that they were angels,
   But to my surprise,
   We climbed aboard their starship,
   We headed for the skies.

Abracadabra

Words and Music by Steve Miller

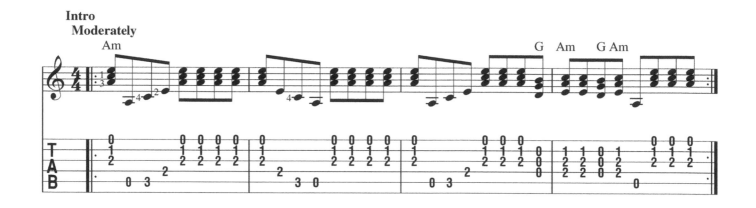

Intro
Moderately

1. I heat up, I can't cool down, you got me spin-nin' a - round and 'round.
3. *See additional lyrics*

'Round and 'round ___ and 'round it goes, ___ where it stops, no-bod-y knows. ___

$\oplus$ Coda

Kiss me, ba - by, let the fire get high - er. _____

Interlude

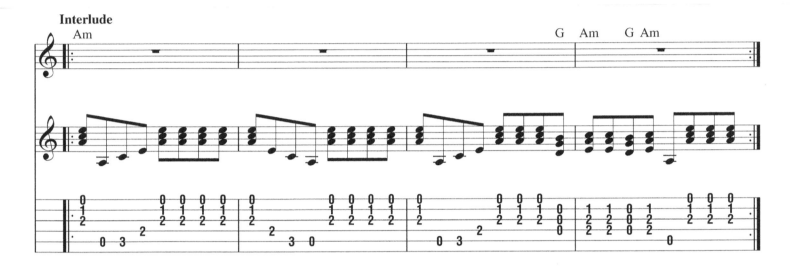

Outro

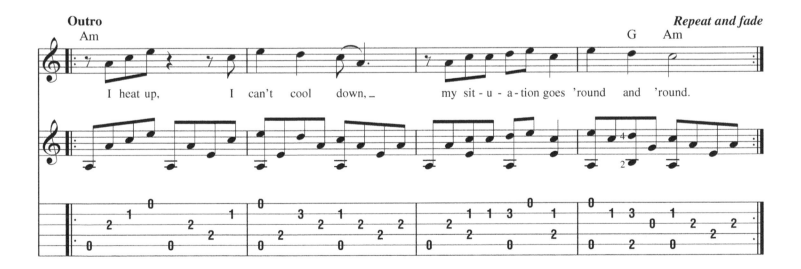

I heat up, I can't cool down, _ my sit - u - a - tion goes 'round and 'round.

Additional Lyrics

3. I feel the magic in your caress.
   I feel magic when I touch your dress.
   Silk and satin, leather and lace,
   Black panties with an angel's face.
   I see the magic in your eyes,
   I hear the magic in your sighs.
   Just when I think I'm gonna get away,
   I hear those words that you always say.

4. Ev'ry time you call my name,
   I heat up like a burnin' flame.
   Burnin' flame, full of desire,
   Kiss me, baby, let the fire get higher.

Brown Eyed Girl

Words and Music by Van Morrison

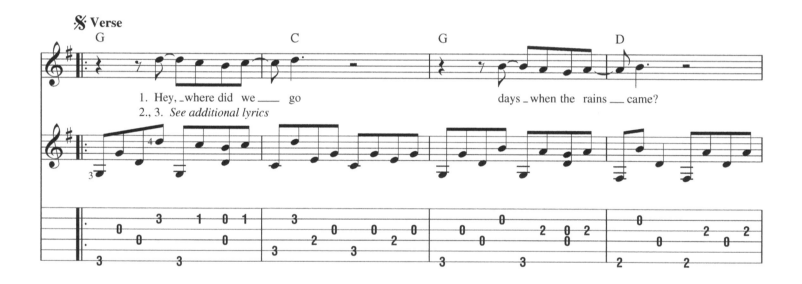

1. Hey, _ where did we _ go   days _ when the rains _ came?
2., 3. *See additional lyrics*

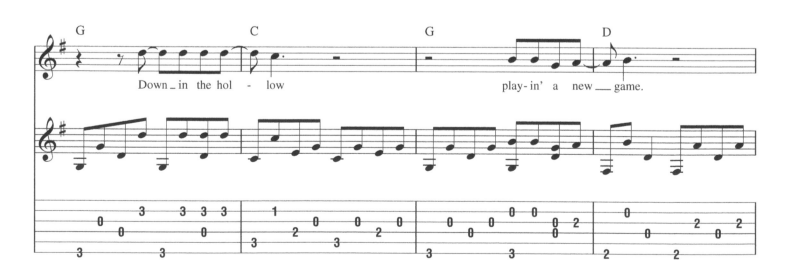

Down _ in the hol - low   play-in' a new _ game.

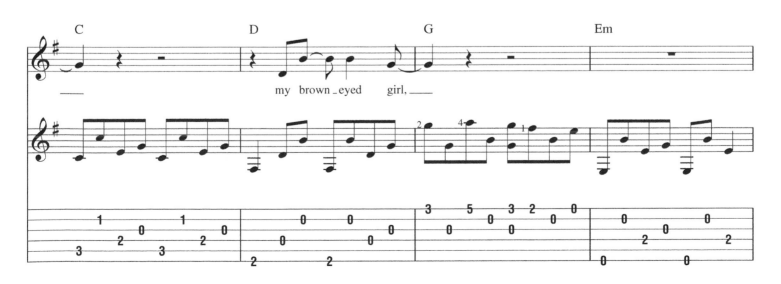

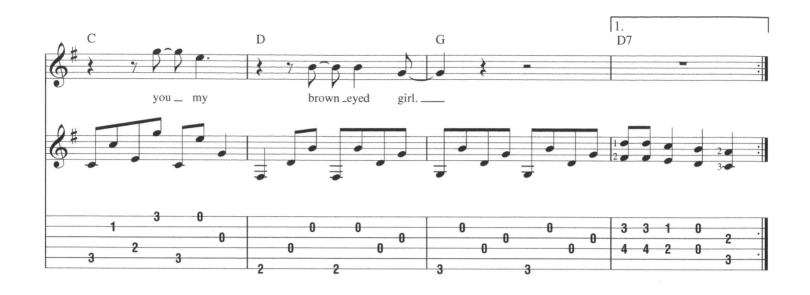

you — my   brown —eyed   girl. —

To Coda ⊕

Do   you   re - mem - ber   when   we   used   to   sing?

Chorus

Sha, la, — la,   la, — la, la, — la,   la, — la,   la, la, te, da. —

14

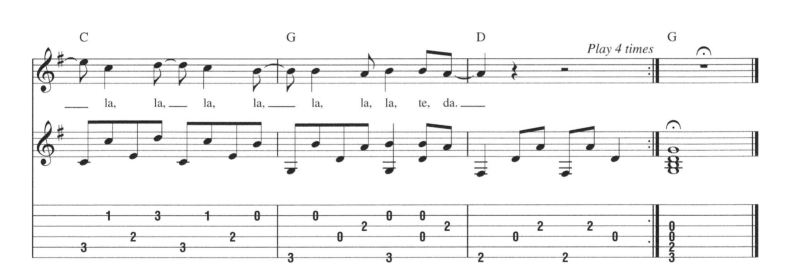

Additional Lyrics

2. Whatever happened
   To Tuesday and so slow,
   Going down the old mine
   With a transistor radio?
   Standing in the sunlight laughin',
   Hidin' behind a rainbow's wall,
   Slippin' and a slidin'
   All along the waterfall with you,
   My brown eyed girl,
   You, my brown eyed girl.

3. So hard to find my way
   Now that I'm on my own.
   I saw you just the other day,
   My, how you have grown.
   Cast my memory back there Lord,
   Sometimes I'm overcome thinkin' 'bout it.
   Makin' love in the green grass
   Behind the stadium with you,
   My brown eyed girl,
   You, my brown eyed girl.

Crocodile Rock

Words and Music by Elton John and Bernie Taupin

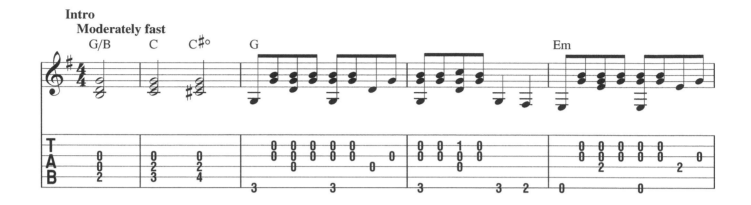

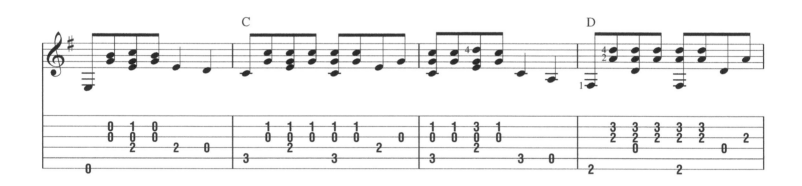

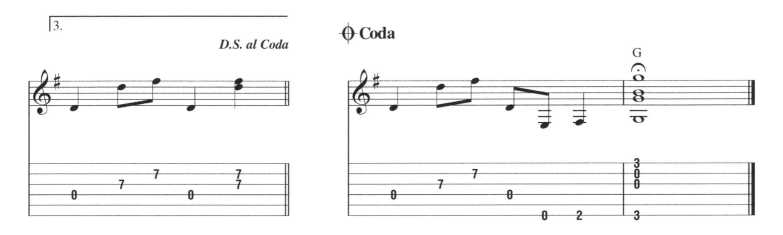

Additional Lyrics

2. But the years went by and rock just died.
   Susie went and left us for some foreign guy.
   Long nights cryin' by the record machine,
   Dreamin' of my Chevy and my old blue jeans.
   But they'll never kill the thrills we got
   Burnin' up to the crocodile rock.
   Learning fast as the weeks went past,
   We really thought the crocodile rock would last.

Free Bird

Words and Music by Allen Collins and Ronnie Van Zant

1. If I leave ___ here to-mor - row, _____
2. *See additional lyrics*

would you ___ still re-mem - ber me?

Well, I must be _____ trav-el-ing on _____ now,

'cause there's too man-y plac _____ es I've ___ got to see.

But if I stay _____ here with ___ you, ___ girl,

things just could-n't be the same.

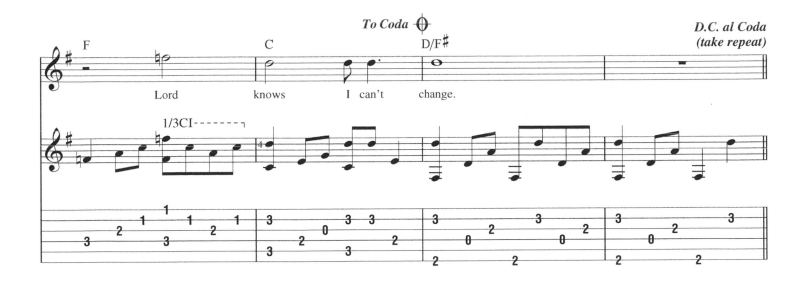

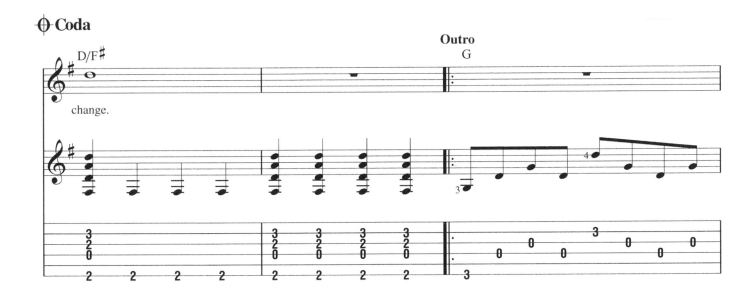

Additional Lyrics

2. Bye bye, baby, it's been a sweet love, yeah, yeah.
   Though this feelin' I can't change.
   A please don't take it so badly,
   'Cause the Lord knows I'm to blame.
   But, if I stay here with you, girl,
   Things just couldn't be the same.
   'Cause I'm as free as a bird now,
   And this bird you cannot change.
   Oh, and a bird you cannot change.
   And this bird you cannot change.
   Lord knows I can't change.

The House of the Rising Sun

Words and Music by Alan Price

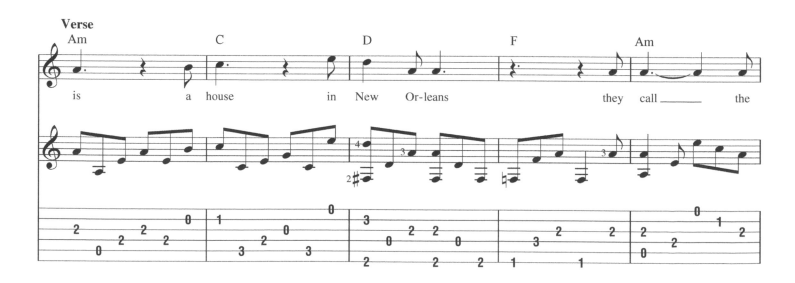

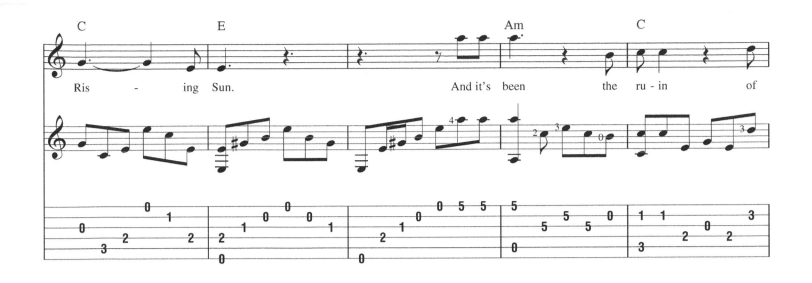

Ris - ing Sun. And it's been the ru - in of

man - y a ___ poor boy, and God, I know I'm one.

man   down _____ in New _____ Or - leans.

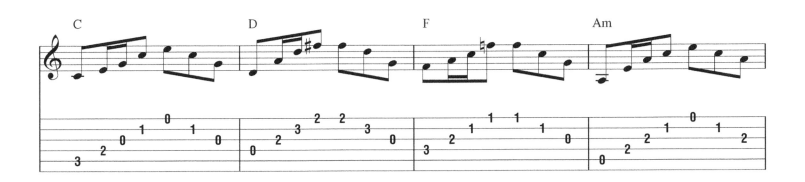

3. Now the

Additional Lyrics

3. Now the only thing a gambler needs
   Is a suitcase and a trunk.
   And the only time he's satisfied
   Is when he's on a drunk.

4. Oh mother, tell your children
   Not to do what I have done;
   Spend your lives in sin and misery
   In the House of the Rising Sun.

5. Well, I got one foot on the platform,
   The other foot on the train.
   I'm goin' back to New Orleans
   To wear that ball and chain.

6. Well, there is a house in New Orleans
   They call the Rising Sun.
   And it's been the ruin of many a poor boy,
   And God, I know I'm one.

Hurts So Good

Words and Music by John Mellencamp and George Green

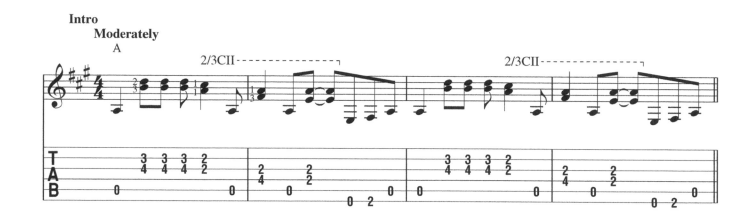

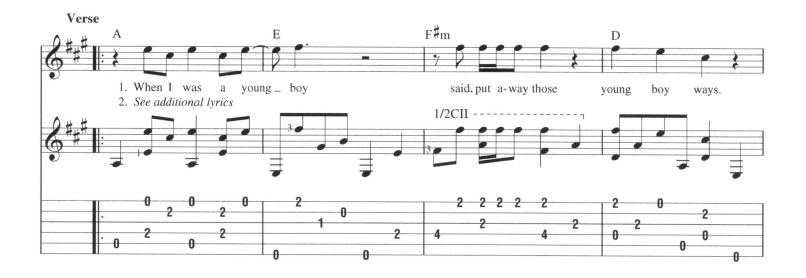

1. When I was a young boy said, put a-way those young boy ways.
2. *See additional lyrics*

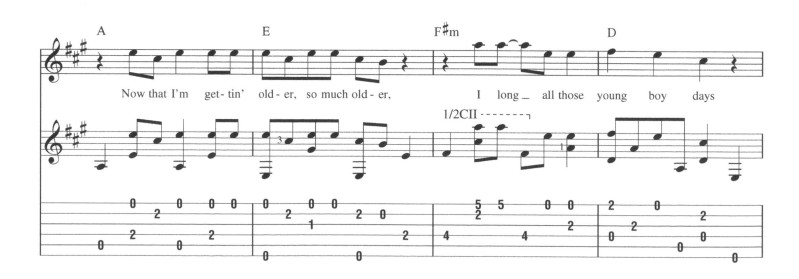

Now that I'm get-tin' old-er, so much old-er, I long all those young boy days

Bridge

I ain't talk-in' no big ___ deals.   I ain't made no   plans ___

___ my - self.   I ain't talk-in' no high ___ heels.   Ba - by, we could ___ walk a - round   all ___

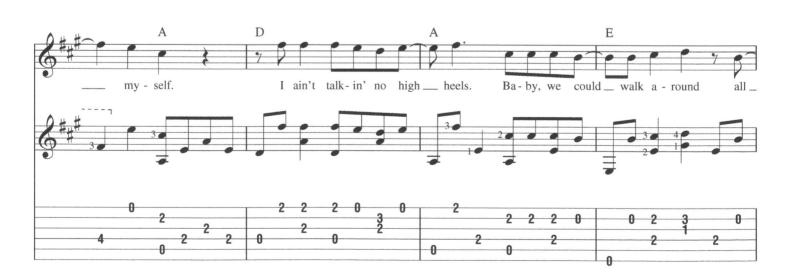

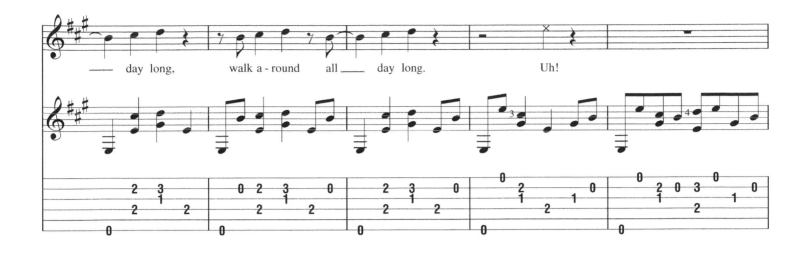

day long,   walk a - round   all ___ day long.   Uh!

D.S. al Coda

✛ **Coda**

Outro

Repeat and fade

Additional Lyrics

2. You don't have to be so excitin'.
Just tryin' to give myself a little bit of fun, yeah.
You always look so invitin'.
You ain't as green as you are young.
Hey, baby, it's you.
Come on, girl, now it's you.
Sink your teeth right through my bones, baby.
Let's see what we can do.
Come on and make it a...

I Want You to Want Me

Words and Music by Rick Nielsen

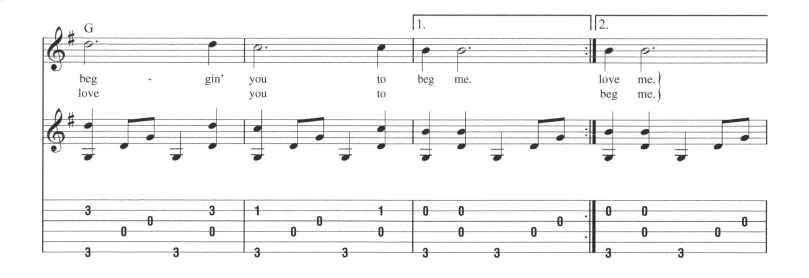

beg - gin' you to beg me.
love you to beg me.
love me.

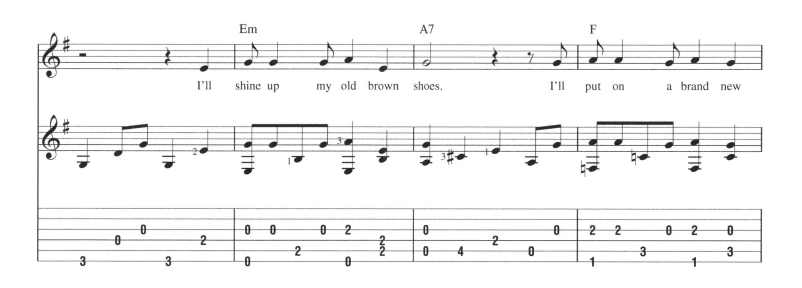

I'll shine up my old brown shoes. I'll put on a brand new

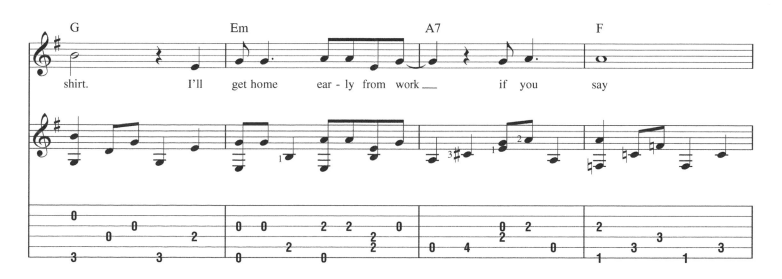

shirt. I'll get home ear - ly from work ___ if you say

33

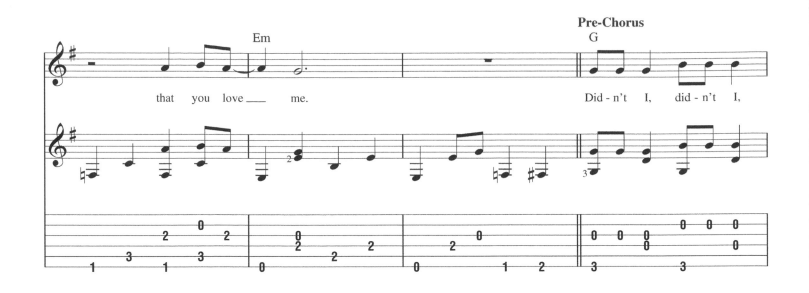

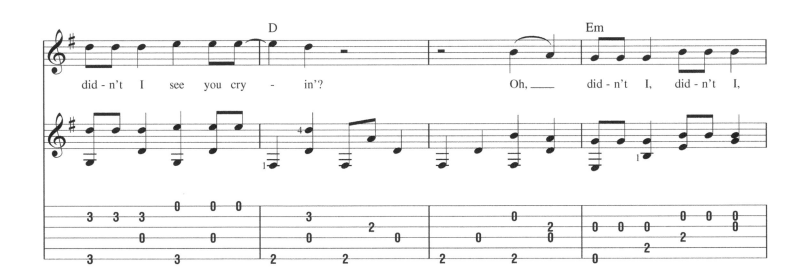

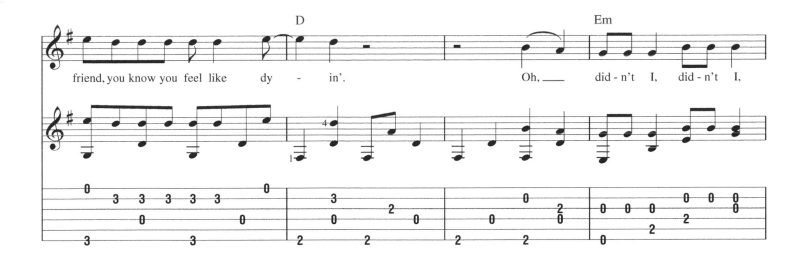

friend, you know you feel like dy - in'.   Oh, ___ did - n't I, did - n't I,

To Coda ⊕   *D.S. al Coda*
                                               (take 2nd ending)

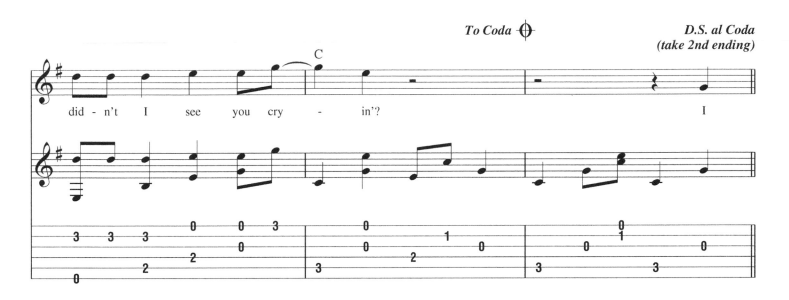

did - n't I see you cry - in'?   I

⊕ **Coda**

Outro

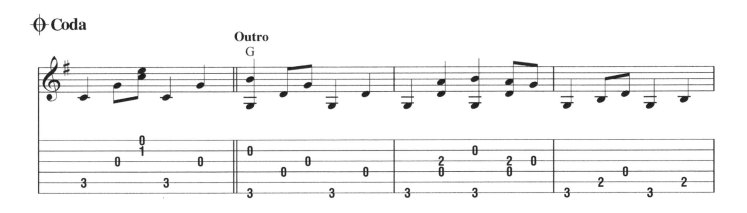

Livin' on a Prayer

Words and Music by Jon Bon Jovi, Richie Sambora and Desmond Child

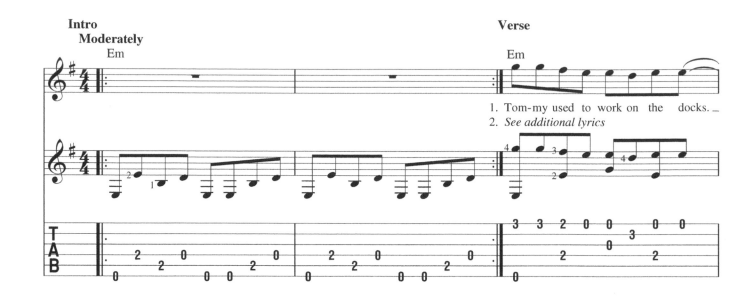

Work-ing for her man, she brings home her pay for love, ____

mmm, for love. _____ She says we've got to

Pre-Chorus

hold on ___ to what we've got. It does-n't make a dif-f'rence if we make it or not. We've

got each oth - er, and that's a lot for ___ love. _ We'll give it a shot.

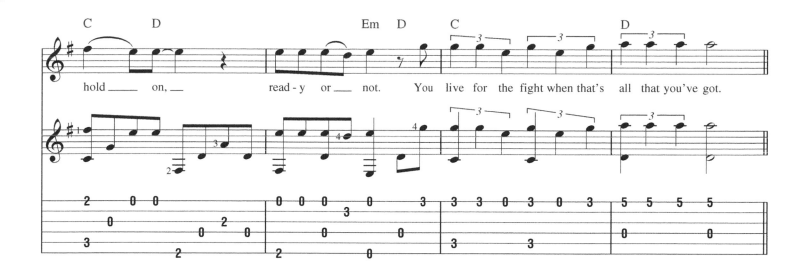

hold _____ on, _____ read-y or ___ not. You live for the fight when that's all that you've got.

Outro-Chorus

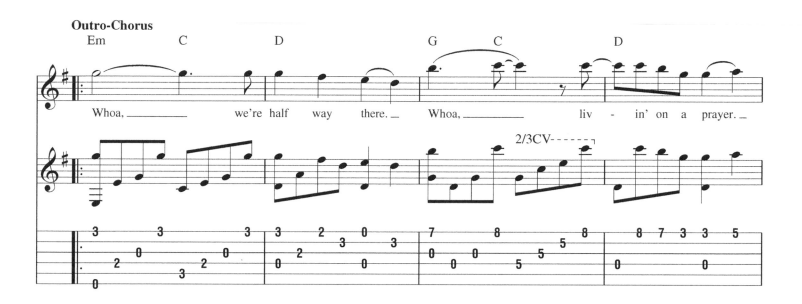

Whoa, _____ we're half way there. ___ Whoa, _____ liv - in' on a prayer. ___

Repeat and fade

Take my ___ hand, ___ we'll make it, I swear. _ Whoa, _____ liv - in' on a prayer. ___

Additional Lyrics

2. Tommy's got his six string in hock.
Now he's holding in when he used to make it talk so tough, mmm, it's tough.
Gina dreams of running away.
When she cries in the night, Tommy whispers, "Baby, it's okay, someday."

Maggie May

Words and Music by Rod Stewart and Martin Quittenton

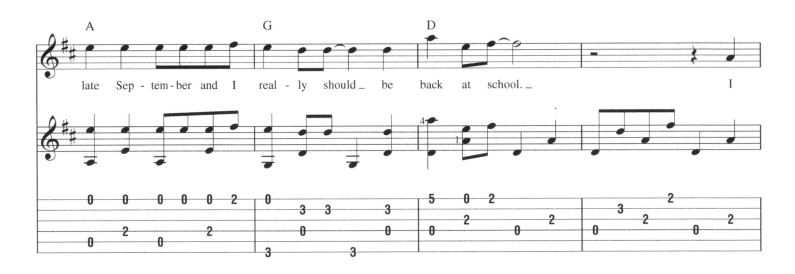

that don't wor-ry me none; __ in my eyes, __ you're ev-'ry-thing. __   I

laughed at all of your jokes. __   My love you did-n't need to coax. __   Oh,

1st time, D.S.
2nd time, D.S. al Coda

Mag-gie, I could-n't have tried __ an-y more. __   2., 3. You

Coda

face. __   You made a first class fool out of me,   but I'm as

Additional Lyrics

Chorus 2. You led me away from home just to save you from being alone.
You stole my soul, and that's a pain I can do without.

3. All I needed was a friend to lend a guiding hand.
But you turned into a lover, and mother what a lover; you wore me out.
All you did was wreck my bed, and in the mornin' kick me in the head.
Oh Maggie, I couldn't have tried any more.

Chorus 3. You led me away from home 'cause you didn't want to be alone.
You stole my heart; I couldn't leave you if I tried.

4. I suppose I could collect my books and get on back to school,
Or steal my daddy's cue and make a living out of playing pool,
Or find myself a rock and roll band that needs a helping hand.
Oh Maggie, I wished I'd never seen your face.
You made a first class fool out of me,
But I was blind as a fool can be.
You stole my heart, but I love you anyway.

Rhiannon

Words and Music by Stevie Nicks

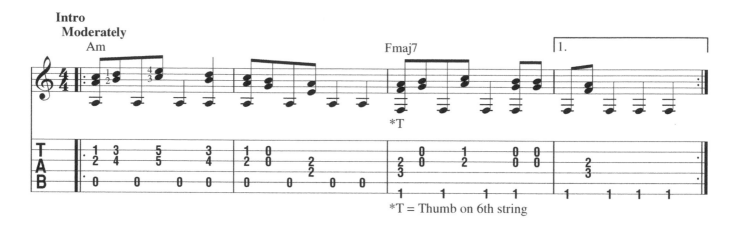

*T = Thumb on 6th string

1. Rhi - an - non rings_ like a bell through the night. And would-n't you love_ to love_

2., 3. *See additional lyrics*

___ her? Takes to the sky like a bird in flight._ And who will be ___ her lov-

Additional Lyrics

2. She is like a cat in the dark.
   And then she is the darkness.
   She rules her life like a flying skylark.
   And when the sky is starlets.

3. She rings like a bell through the night.
   And wouldn't you love to love her?
   She rules her life like a bird in flight.
   And who will be her lover?

Still the Same

Words and Music by Bob Seger

1. You al - ways won, __
2. *See additional lyrics*

ev - 'ry - time you placed a bet. __

You're

still damn good, ___ no one's got-ten to you yet. ___

Ev - 'ry time ___ they were sure they had you caught, ___

you were quick - er than they thought. _____

You'd just turn your back and walk. ___

2. You

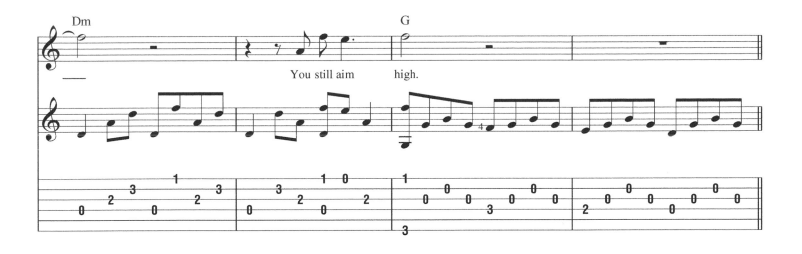

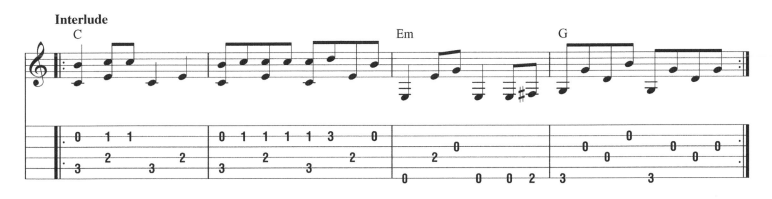

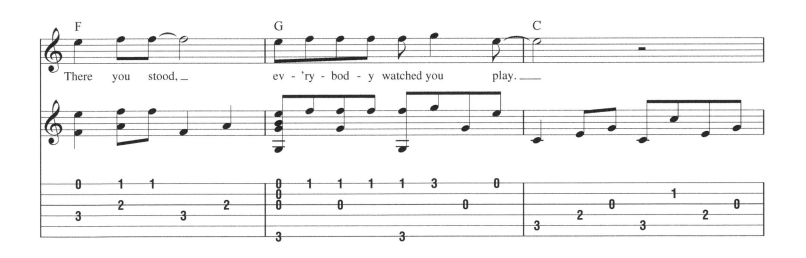

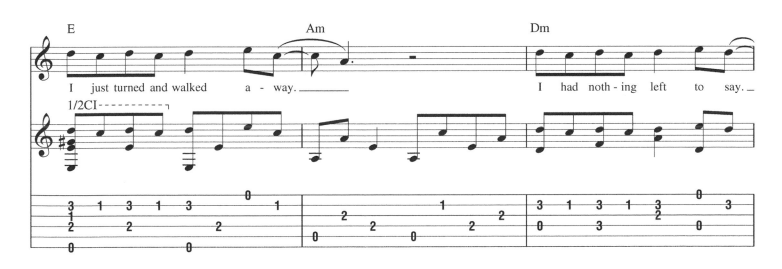

Outro

'Cause you're still the same. __

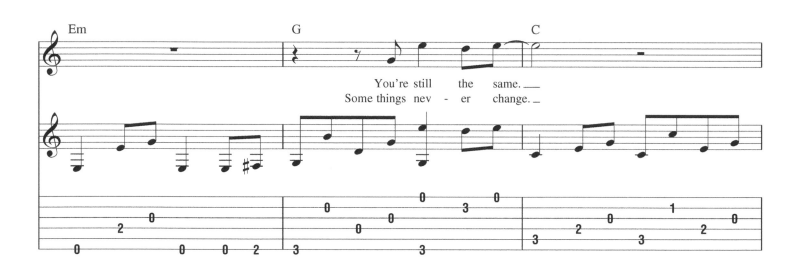

You're still the same. __
Some things nev - er change. _

Repeat and fade

Mov - in' game to game. __
You're still the same. __

Additional Lyrics

2. You always said, the cards would never do you wrong.
   The trick, you said, was never play the game too long.
   A gambler's share, the only risk that you would take,
   The only loss you could forsake,
   The only bluff you couldn't fake.

When the Children Cry

Words and Music by Mike Tramp and Vito Bratta

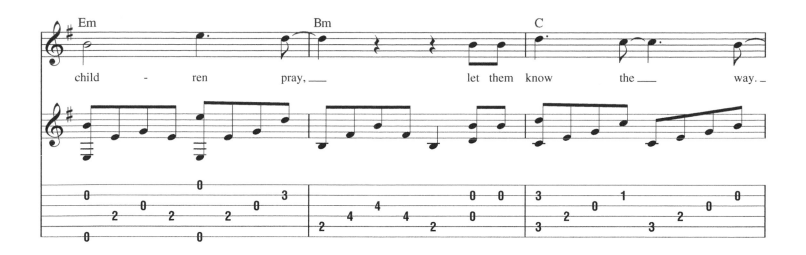

child - ren pray, ___ let them know the ___ way. _

_ 'Cause when the child - ren sing, ___ then the

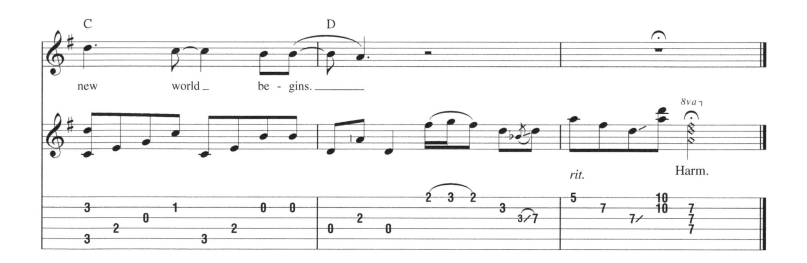

new world _ be - gins. _____

rit. Harm.

Additional Lyrics

2. Little child, you must show the way
   To a better day for all the young.
   'Cause you were born for the world to see
   That we all can live with love and peace.

Pre-Chorus No more presidents, and all the wars will end.
   One united world under God.

Wheel in the Sky

Words and Music by Robert Fleischman, Neal Schon and Diane Valory

Verse

1. Win-ter is here __ a - gain, __ oh Lord. Have-n't been home __ in a
2. *See additional lyrics*

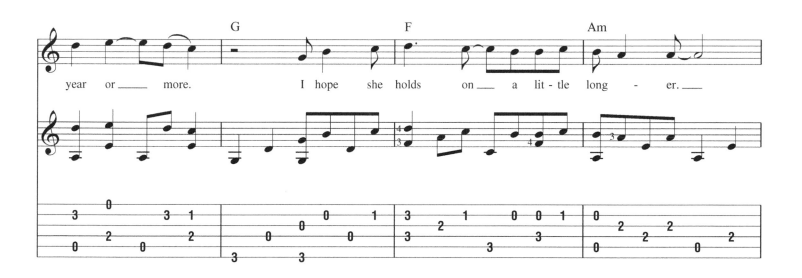

year or __ more. I hope she holds on __ a lit-tle long - er. __

Sent a let-ter on a long sum-mer day made of sil - ver,

not of clay. ____ Oo, I've been run - nin' down _ this dust - y road. ____

% Chorus

__ Oo, the wheel in the sky keeps on turn - in'. I don't know where I'll be to -

mor - row. ____ Wheel in the sky keeps on turn - in'.

To Coda ⊕ | 1.

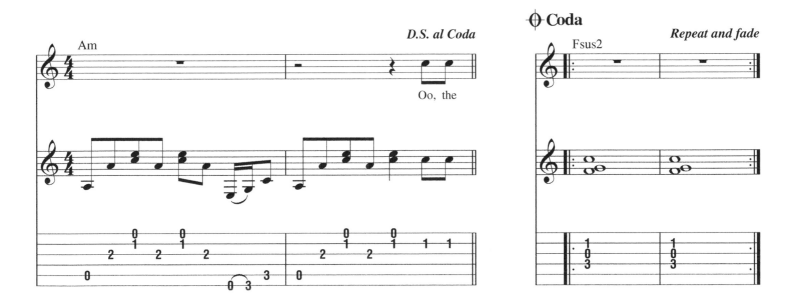

Additional Lyrics

2. I've been tryin' to make it home.
   Got to make it before too long.
   Oo, I can't take this very much longer, no.
   I'm stranded in the sleet and rain.
   Don't think I'm ever gonna make it home again.
   The mornin' sun is risin',
   It's kissin' the day.

White Room

Words and Music by Jack Bruce and Pete Brown

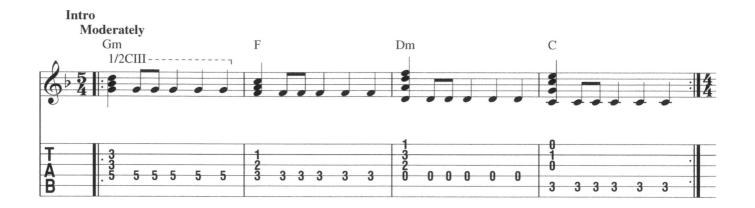

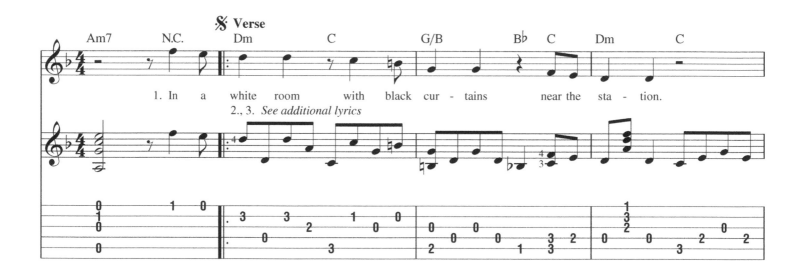

1. In a white room with black cur - tains near the sta - tion.

2., 3. *See additional lyrics*

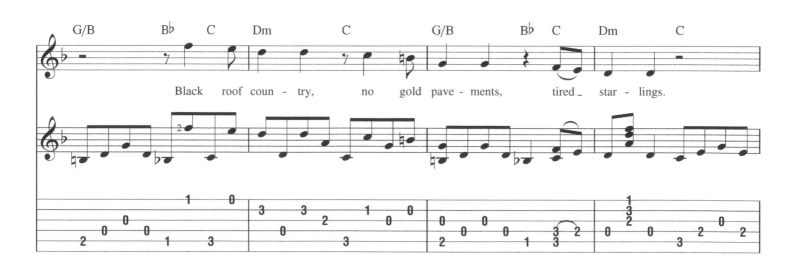

Black roof coun - try, no gold pave - ments, tired _ star - lings.

Additional Lyrics

2. You said no strings could secure you at the station.
Platform ticket, restless diesel, goodbye windows.
I walked into such a sad time at the station.
As I walked out, felt my own need just beginning.

3. At the party, she was kindness in the hard crowd.
Isolation for the old queen now forgotten.
Yellow tigers crouched in jungles in her dark eyes.
She's just dressing goodbye windows, tired starling.

Bridge 2. I'll wait in the queue when the trains come back.
Lie with you where the shadows run from themselves.

Bridge 3. I'll sleep in this place with the lonely crowd.
Lie in the dark where the shadows run from themselves.